"To strive, to seek, to find, and not to yield"

Contents

About the Author

DR KEVIN DONNELLY taught for 18 years in government and non-government schools after attending Broadmeadows High and Melbourne High and graduating from La Trobe University in 1974.

He is one of Australia's leading education authors and commentators and Director of Melbourne-based Education Standards Institute.

Kevin writes on a regular basis for Australia's print media, including: *The Australian*, the *Herald Sun*, the *Courier Mail*, *The Age* and the *Sydney Morning Herald*. He also appears regularly on radio and TV.

Previous books include *Why our Schools are Failing*, *Dumbing Down: the Impact of the Culture Wars on our Schools*, *Australia's Education Revolution* and *Educating Your Child: It's Not Rocket Science*.

Kevin has also contributed chapters to a number of books on education and public policy issues including: *What if?*, *The Greens: Policies, Reality and Consequences*, *Really Dangerous Ideas*, *Future Proofing Australia* and *Turning Left or Right: Values in Modern Politics*.

After growing up in Broadmeadows Kevin now lives in Surrey Hills (Victoria) and is married to Julia and children include James and Amelia. Pastimes include travelling to Indo-China, enjoying Australian wine, shopping at the Victoria market, walking with Julia and reading biographies and making homemade pasta and pizza.

Foreword

This small personal volume, if it helps just one person through a time of unexpected hardship or grief, will have served its purpose.

Grief, loss, hardship unaddressed can often lead to serious depression and illness.

No one suggests such episodes are easy to deal with, they are not, but address them we must and move on with our lives.

In this book Kevin address his personal experiences in youth, with family, and then the death of his only son James. The difficulties in dealing with James's death, Kevin's depression and his realisation that life must go on.

James will never be forgotten, or his contribution to family and friends lessened.

But those left behind must live, and live the life that James would have wanted family and friends to lead.

Kevin Donnelly's experience could be faced by any of us at any time.

Read on.

Jeff Kennett AC
Chairman
beyondblue
The National Depression Initiative

Introduction

Depression: Australia's comic genius Spike Milligan suffered from it, the Australian Liberal Party politician Andrew Robb took time off parliament because of it and Winston Churchill described it as his black dog.

Surveys and research prove that it is a widespread and ever present problem afflicting millions across the world. For all of Western society's promise of material happiness and fulfilment the record sales of antidepressants and rates of suicide and mental illness prove that something is seriously amiss.

It's a weekly event to hear about post-traumatic stress and that those in harms way – including soldiers, fire fighters, police and ambulance drivers – are in need of grief counselling and guidance.

Depression is especially prevalent among men. Based on the Australian Bureau of Statistics figures for 2009, 77% of those committing suicide in Australia were men (a total of 2,132) making it the 10th most common cause of death among males.

Women, on the other hand, have a much lower incidence of suicide based on the 2009 figures. The rate for females is 4.4 deaths per 100,000 compared to 14.9 out of 100,000 for males.

A 2013 survey carried out by the Young and Well Co-operative Research Centre revealed that the problem of depression and suicide is especially prevalent among young men aged 16-25. The survey revealed that 27% were worried about depression, one in five felt life had little purpose and 40% said they were experiencing psychological distress.

The following is an account of my experience of depression and the reality, no matter how much we try and manage our fate and protect those around us, there are forces beyond our control and events that we cannot influence.

We are all individuals with our own unique psychological makeup and past experience and we are all tested and challenged in different ways. Some lose loved ones, some are victims of family violence, some are abused and some witness and experience events that cause a loss of faith and destroy any sense of optimism for the future.

At the same time, not all is bleak and destructive. Along with suffering and self-doubt is the ability to be resilient in the face of adversity. Churchill's black dog might be an ever-present companion but, to admit as such does not deny that life continues and that happiness and fulfilment are still achievable.

As proven by countless artists, musicians, actors, comedians and successful public figures, it is also possible to channel depression into something positive, and while nothing will ever be the same, to live a life worth living and to keep the black dog at bay.

For Spike Milligan it was writing poetry, for Andrew Robb early morning swims and for England's war-time Prime Minister it was painting and working in his garden.

For me, as for many others, the myths, fables and legends of early childhood prove an invaluable help in confronting hopelessness and despair. Romantic heroes like *Beowulf, Sinbad the Sailor* and *Odysseus* overcome personal trials by showing courage and resourcefulness.

That so many Hollywood films like *Troy*, *Clash of the Titans, Thor* and *Immortals* are based on classical mythology prove how enduring such archetypal stories are and how they appeal to deep seated emotional and psychological needs.

Comic book heroes like Superman, Batman and Iron Man also play a part in teaching about bravery and not giving in while all might seem hopeless. The criticism that such figures are often one-dimensional, while true, doesn't deny that young boys, in particular, need strong role models to emulate.

Girls, too, need strong role models; I remember reading my daughter Amelia stories about the Celtic queen Boudica who fought valiantly and bravely against the Roman invaders. Add mythical figures like the Amazons, modern day heroines like the aviatrix Amelia Earhart and Australia's Nancy Wake and girls will learn that they can overcome adversity and beat the odds.

Literature provides a rich and enduring source of understanding that helps deal with tragic and unexpected fate. Greek tragedies like *Oedipus the King* and *Medea* prepare one to understand that the gods are not always just and that to be human is to be vulnerable.

Shakespeare's plays like *King Lear*, *Hamlet* and *Macbeth* also teach how we cannot escape destiny and that our thoughts and actions, no matter how much we might believe are justified, can have destructive, far reaching consequences.

Lines like: "There's a divinity that shapes our ends, Rough hew them how we will" and "As flies to wanton boys are we to the gods: They kill us for their sport" emphasise that life can be cruel and unpredictable.

At the same time, literature can enthuse about the potential to live life to the full, to gain from the experience and find a deeper sense of satisfaction and contentment. While now politically incorrect, larger than life and effusive characters like Zorba from *Zorba the Greek* display an infectious zest for living based on music, dance and physical appetites.

In David Malouf's *Fly Away Peter*, the end of the novella suggests that there is a continuity and purpose in life that transcends the pain and loss caused by death. For most of the time, we skate across the surface of things, but literature often enables us to discover a more complex, profound and transcendent sense of existence.

Music, sculpture, dance and art can also transport one to a sublime and moving world that refreshes one's perception of life and that helps one address ever present, existential questions about life and death, happiness and despondency and the best way to live one's life and find fulfilment.

As I was raised as a Catholic, religious faith also provides a strong counter weight to depression and despair. Original sin and Christ's suffering on the cross point to the belief that this life, in many ways, is 'a vale of tears'. At the same time, Christ's resurrection and God's unconditional love tells us that there is a spiritual world offering solace and "the peace that passeth all understanding".

The words of the Christian mystic, Julian of Norwich – "All shall be well, and all shall be well, and all manner of things shall be well" – also point to the belief that we are not forsaken. T.S. Eliot makes use of these lines in *Little Gidding V* when he writes:

> *And all shall be well and*
> *All manner of things shall be well*
> *When the tongues of flame are in-folded*

Into the crowned knot of fire
And the fire and the rose are one.

While there are many sceptics in what is becoming an increasingly secular world, the reality is that Christianity is not alone in arguing that there is a higher purpose in life. Buddhism and Hinduism, for example, tell us that this life is a 'veil of illusion' and their teachings provide a path to a deeper awareness and sense of truth.

The Zen saying 'chop wood, carry water', as well as suggesting the need for mindfulness and living the moment as fully as possible, also suggests that it is important to appreciate the value of what might appear to be menial tasks and the way physical activity can refresh the spirit.

Sometimes, instead of dwelling on self-pity it is better to throw yourself into something active and to live in the moment, enjoying the satisfaction that comes from mastering something difficult or the simple pleasure of being exhausted.

The love, compassion and understanding of family and friends are also vital in buoying one and proving that all is not lost. For me, a wife and daughter not only provide a reason to overcome adversity but, more importantly, their sympathy, affection and warmth provide a beacon of happiness and hope.

For men, in particular, it is also vital to be true to one's emotions and feelings and to be open and not afraid to reveal weakness; especially to other men. The danger with conforming to the male stereotype of always being in control and appearing brave is that the façade belies underlying doubts and fears.

If not expressed or dealt with, such feelings of despondency and emptiness can be destructive and life threatening. Men must also guard against reacting violently against those who are closest in a futile attempt to assuage their suffering and grief.

Alcohol and drugs, while providing temporary relief, only mask what is ever present and exacerbate what can be an ever-spiralling descent into depression and despair. As every alcoholic knows, getting drunk never solves the problem and the pain and emptiness are still there the morning after.

I once believed that life was full of optimism and joy and that pain and suffering only happened to others. I now know that very few of us go through life untouched and unscathed. At the same time I've slowly come to realise, like many others, that pain and suffering tempers us, that we can overcome adversity and that there is still much to live for.

The final line from Tennyson's poem *Ulysses*, quoted by M in the James Bond movie *Skyfall*, best sums it up. Instead of giving in to fate and our fears and anxieties, we need:

"To strive, to seek, to find, and not to yield"

Thank you to those who read and responded to drafts, including Julia Donnelly, my sister in law Sylvia Johnson and friends and acquaintances: Tess Livingstone, Shelley Gare, Heather Marmur, Cresside Collette, Nicky Peters, Michelle Longland, Sophie Masson, Pippa Masson, Sally Brooks, Hamish Brooks, Shelly Gare, Ros Chandler and Ross Fitzgerald.

Also, thank you to Kate Zappner for her time and skill in editing the book and for offering suggestions for improvement and to Jeff Kennett for agreeing to write the preface.

As always, as the author I take responsibility for any mistakes and for what follows. I can be contacted at kevind@ netspace.net.au.

If you or someone you know is depressed please contact Lifeline Australia on 13 11 14 or beyondblue on 1300 22 4636 to seek professional advice and support.

Part 1

Childhood

Growing up in a Housing Commission house in Broadmeadows wasn't easy but, luckily, nobody told us that at the time.

Yes, we were at the end of the suburban train line, we lacked services like cinemas and hospitals, the grog was a problem and many struggled below the poverty line, but as children, we had no idea that we should feel sorry for ourselves or that being working class equated with disadvantage.

The dunny-can man carried the night soil away in the early hours of the morning and whenever the horse pulling the dairy cart left his calling card, we would rush to be the first to collect the manure for the garden.

Not that we had much of a garden, or lawn for that matter. In the 60s, Melbourne's urban sprawl had yet to spiral out of control and much of Broadmeadows was still country: with thistle-infected, basalt plains, rabbit warrens, the Bulla Creek, blue-tongue lizards to catch and trees to climb.

A perfect playground for children raised before computers, the internet, Facebook, YouTube, computer games, mobile phones and helicopter parents – always hovering around wrapping children in cotton wool and suffocating them with parental concern.

Broadmeadows may have been a rough area but there was

a strong sense of community and a strict sense of morality when it came to children – anyone who transgressed was soon dealt with. As kids, we felt safe and were allowed to take risks, push the boundaries and generally roam free.

On summer weekends, we would check the tyres on our Malvern Star bikes, splash a bit of oil on the chain and head off, cross-country to Bulla Creek. As the youngest, I was last in line as the older boys peddled furiously ahead, without helmets, swerving around rocks and launching off mounds of dirt.

Like all country creeks, ours had an old, gnarled tree, leaning over a bend in the river, with a rope attached. The hardest part was to grab the rope at the right place as you launched yourself into space – too low and your backside scraped along the ground, too high and you lost momentum and failed to reach the deepest part of the creek.

Behind our house was the St Joseph's baby home, bordered by tall, straight pine trees. Our favourite dare was to see how high you could climb or how far out on a limb you could crawl before gravity asserted itself and cold fear grew in the pit of your stomach. Being small framed and light in weight, I always had the best chance of winning.

Each major branch was named after a Melbourne street – Spring, Elizabeth and Collins – and the higher branches made a perfect possie from which to drop a pine cone on someone below and to keep a look out for the local groundsman.

After school, time was spent kicking a football made of tightly wrapped newspaper, tied with string, or playing cricket in the middle of the road, with a rusty dustbin as stumps. One of the better off kids had a real cricket bat but, whenever he was given out, he would spit the dummy and literally take his bat and go home.

Long hot, summer days were spent at the local swimming pool, where we tanned ourselves, did water bombs, and when bored, caught and picked the wings off flies. We had yet to be warned about skin cancer and far too often mum had to bathe my back in vinegar to sooth my burnt, peeling skin.

Guy Fawkes' night, otherwise known as cracker night, was the highlight of the year. Unlike now, when crackers are illegal and almost impossible to find, we were overwhelmed with choice. Penny Bangers, Rockets, Tom Thumbs, Catherine Wheels and Sparklers competed as we tried to outdo one another with the most imaginative, and often risky, way of exploiting our arsenal.

One dare was to see if you could hold a cracker at arm's length and not let it drop as it was about to explode; while another was to see who had the cheek to blow up a neighbour's letterbox. My favourite was blowing the old garbage can onto the roof of the house with a couple of Penny Bangers tied together.

Life was a lot simpler back then. On Saturdays we'd help mum with the laundry involving an old copper boiler, concrete trough and hand wringer – the bed sheets were the hardest and you needed a strong arm to get them through the wringer.

Every night after dinner, my older brother Gordon and I would take it in turn to dry the dishes and it was only years later that I discovered that automatic dishwashers were increasingly commonplace in more affluent suburbs. Standing next to mum gave us the chance to talk over the day's events and for her to quiz us about what was happening at school.

Long before we had heard the word multiculturalism, we lived in a community surrounded by different languages and different histories. After the war, a migrant hostel had been set up in the grounds of the Broadmeadows Army Camp and the local schools enrolled children from London, Glasgow, Athens and the Ukraine.

On one corner opposite our house in Gibson Street lived the Heinz's, a family that had emigrated from Germany, on the other corner my friend Ken Lee Tet and at school my friends included Nick Shilo and Agathias Argyropoulos.

Part 2

Early Years

One of the most vivid images I have is running along Gibson Street, pushing a trolley after working at the local milk bar. I was happy for no other reason than because I was young, it was a warm, clear summer evening and I was on the way home.

I needed the trolley early the following morning to collect newspapers from the railway station and drop them off at the shop before walking to school. Gordon and I worked in the local milk bar most of the week before or after school and on weekends filling fridges, collecting papers and stacking empty bottles.

I earned $252.82 cents in one financial year – not bad for a 15 year old doing part time work when the weekly minimum wage was about $37.

Schools were different then. Discipline was strict, students were streamed in terms of ability, teachers were smartly dressed and authority was respected. At assemblies we stood to attention, sang the national anthem as the flag was raised, and with hand on our hearts, recited the oath of allegiance:

I'll love God and my Country
I'll honour the flag
I'll serve the Queen
And cheerfully obey

My parents, teachers and the law

As they say, the past is a foreign country, and late 50s and early to-mid 60s predated Woodstock, anti-Vietnam moratoriums, flower power and the contraceptive pill. Sir Robert Menzies had been Australia's Prime Minister for nearly 16 years, Australia was a proud member of the Commonwealth and children were told to be seen and not heard.

I still remember the old school exercise books with a world map on the back with the British Empire coloured in red – stretching across the globe from east to west, north and south.

I also remember the Liverpudlian physical education teacher who would invite any boy causing trouble in class to meet him behind the shelter shed after school to 'discuss' matters, needless to say, classroom behaviour was not a major problem.

The school had an imaginary line drawn dividing it in half with girls on one side and boys on the other. At recess and lunchtime the rule was 'no mixing' and girls and boys stayed in their allotted area – the one exception being the toilet block were there was always a chance of sneaking a word or two over the drinking trough.

Once a week at assembly the girls had the length of their dresses measured, and I remember, on one occasion and much to our disappointment, the latest fashion in girls' knickers witches britches being banned.

Lunchtime was spent playing British Bulldog or Brandy and scraped knees and the odd bruise were all part of growing up. This was a time long before schools banned physical games like stacks on the mill because of worried parents or the fear of litigation.

In the senior years there were etiquette and dancing classes where the boys learned to be courteous and how to dance the Pride of Erin – not too close, one hand in the middle of your partner's back and don't look down at your feet. The girls were taught deportment and how to make conversation.

Unlike today, where children and adolescents are surrounded by sexuality and promiscuity, ours was a more innocent time. Girlie magazines where hidden under the counter, popular culture had yet to succumb to crude song lyrics and explicit sexuality and celebrities still maintained a sense of respectability.

I'll never forget when one of the boys brought a pen to school depicting a woman in a bathing suit who revealed her nakedness when the pen was turned upside down. At Mass we learned that it was a sin to look at a girl or a woman with impure thoughts and to let the devil have his way.

My favourite place was the library, where I would disappear at lunchtime, hunting for the latest Ray Bradbury short story or the next in the Wyndham science-fiction series. Greek myths and Norse fables were also a favourite – stories of valour, ingenuity and mortality.

Countless hours were spent before the walls of Troy, listening to fierce battle cries and the noise of clashing arms. Many more hours were spent journeying with Odysseus on his way back to Ithaca; a return fraught with danger and calamity and only overcome with resourcefulness and strength.

Reading about Narcissus, Pandora's Box, Icarus and Beowulf vanquishing the Grendel ignited my imagination and provided an exciting world in which I could escape.

It was years later after reading Joseph Campbell that I

realised the lasting value of the legends, archetypes and myths that I had been introduced to when at school. No wonder George Lucas based much of the *Star Wars* films on his discussions with Campbell about the eternal struggle between the good and the dark side of the force.

Emotional and psychological resilience do not happen by accident, the reservoir from which we draw when dealing with pain and adversity is part of a larger spiritual world that is ever present.

Throw in Shakesepeare, Dickens and the poetry of Judith Wright and Kenneth Slessor and you have the beginnings of a life-long enjoyment of literature. Thankfully, this was a time when the classics were centre stage and nobody had yet to argue that working class kids should spend their time reading comics, popular magazines and graffiti.

It was also a time before surfing the net, texting and ever flickering electronic screens, when children still knew how to escape into the world of the imagination and empathise with larger than life characters and be transported to past worlds and foreign lands.

Long before progressive education fads like creative writing and whole language, Mr Clayton taught us the rules of grammar and syntax, précis and how to parse a sentence. Most likely, if he had been asked, Mr Clayton would have agreed with what Winston Churchill, the British war-time Prime Minister, had to say about mastering the English language. Churchill writes about his time at school:

> *Not only did we learn English parsing thoroughly, but we also practised continually English analysis... Thus I got into my bones the essential structure of the ordinary British sentence – which is a noble thing.*

Another teacher, Mr Mackie, organised lunch time screenings of Shakespearean plays like *Richard III* and *Hamlet* where we were transported to a world full of drama, conflict and rich and evocative language.

Mr Mackie also began a hiking club where we were challenged by overnight adventures on Victoria's high plains. Sleeping rough in the open air, learning basic bush craft and marvelling at the majestic beauty and tranquillity of snow capped mountains, again, introduced us to a world far from the Housing Commission estate in which we were growing up.

The school also had a science club where we were allowed to borrow a small, portable telescope. I remember spending many nights on the house roof waiting expectedly to catch the sight of a meteor streaking across the night sky or gazing at the sundrenched surface of the moon.

Most Saturdays, a group of us met in a nearby church in a book group organised by the local Anglican priest. While the names and titles were foreign to us – Fromm's *The Art of Loving*, Lorenz's *On Aggression*, C. S. Lewis' *The Screwtape Letters* and the works of Plato and Socrates – I still savour the excitement and reward I felt as a result of the experience.

This was a time, before all the talk about working-class kids being disadvantaged and unable to cope, when teachers, priests and others believed that the best way to help was to challenge and extend us academically and to enrich our world with enduring arguments and ideas.

Comics, *Mad* magazine, black and white TV and pop groups like the Beach Boys and the Beatles were also on the agenda as I entered adolescence. While now politically incorrect, I remember war comics where courageous, bronzed diggers fought along the Kokoda Track against the evil Jap who fought without honour or respect for the defenceless.

The Walt Disney show was essential viewing every Sunday night and we were such addicts that we ended up knowing more about Buffalo Bill, Davey Crocket and the War of Independence than our home grown heroes and Australia's history as a nation.

The good news is that Disney also introduced us to classical music with productions like *Fantasia* with Mickey Mouse as the Sorcerer's apprentice.

One year, I remember watching ballet on ABC TV – small, graceful black and white figures moving effortlessly across the stage, the ballerinas fine and elegant and the men physically stronger but no less artistic. A world of music, beauty and the sublime opened up to me – a world that I was to revisit and find solace as I grew older.

Many nights, after footy training, dinner and homework, I would lie in bed listening on my transistor radio to Johnny O'Keefe, Petula Clark and the Animals.

In 1967, a group of us wagged school to listen to the just released Beatles' album *Sgt. Pepper's Lonely Hearts Club Band.* We spent all afternoon arguing about the lyrics in Lucy in the Sky with Diamonds and whether the song was drug inspired.

On the nightly TV news we saw images of soldiers traversing rice fields, exploding napalm and placard waving demonstrators. The anti-war movement was growing and while we were too young to fully understand what was happening, many of the songs we listened to spoke of peace, solidarity and the need to question authority.

Childhood was also a time of growing up as a Catholic – baptism, communion, confirmation and a church calendar celebrating a yearly cycle of birth, death, resurrection, redemption, forgiveness and salvation. Each night, my brother and I would kneel by our beds and pray. I still remember the lines:

Now I lay me down to sleep
I pray to God my soul to keep
If I die before I wake
I pray to God my soul to take

I also remember as a child in bed sheltering under my blanket, holding on to an incandescent statue of the Virgin Mary. In her presence I sought comfort and safety and I knew that if she moved, miracles existed and that I would be saved.

On Sunday mum would take us to St Dominic's where we sat obediently as the priest recited the Latin Mass and the smell of incense wafted through the church. This was a time before Vatican II, when the priest stood facing the altar with his back to the congregation and liberation theology had yet to question established truths.

The parables from the *Bible* taught lessons about courage, forgiveness, resisting evil and temptation and choosing what was good. Following Christ on his journey to the cross we sympathised with his suffering and sacrifice and appreciated how he gave up his life that we should be saved.

While mum was a Catholic, dad on the other hand, was a member of the Communist Party and enlisted us in the Eureka Youth Movement where we learned about Lenin, Uncle Joe and Chairman Mao. He worked at the railway's Newport Workshops that, I later found out, was a centre for left-wing, radical politics after the Labor Split of the mid 1950s.

Here we were taught the Communist maxim, 'from each

according to his ability, to each according to his needs', and celebrated events like the Eureka Stockade where the oppressed miners fought against injustice and tyranny.

Dad's great grandfather, John Donnelly, had emigrated from King's Country, Ireland in 1841 and settled in country NSW close to what is now known as the town of Wagga Wagga. The family eventually owned over one million and a half acres, according to one source, and during the more profitable times Tom Donnelly donated 40 acres, valued at 1,500 pounds, to the Presentation Sisters to allow them to build a convent.

Unfortunately, dad never inherited anything. By the time he was born the 1890s depression, rabbit plagues and the demon drink, otherwise known as the Irish disease, had long destroyed the family's fortunes.

Mum's ancestry was also Irish-Catholic and, like dad, she had strong connections to the land. Her father's side descended from Arthur Wellington who had been born in 1849 in what is now known as Horsham. He lived and worked most of his life in the Wimmera and mum grew up in Seymour before settling in Melbourne.

Dad also read us Banjo Paterson and Henry Lawson and instilled in us the belief that working men and women are the salt of the earth and not beholden to those who considered themselves superior because of birth, wealth or privilege. I still remember dad swearing at a flickering, black and white TV image of Prime Minister Menzies and abusing him as 'pig iron Bob'.

The Catholic social and political activist B. A. Santamaria, who I was fortunate enough to meet a number of times before he died, once told me I was very lucky to have a Catholic mother and a Communist father. What better way to understand the significance of the ongoing conflict between one of the 20th Century's most influential ideologies and the teachings of the Church.

Part 3

Father Departs

S ome nights, after falling asleep, I felt my body slowly lift from my bed and hover above the rooftops. The feeling was one of weightlessness and freedom. Looking down on the houses and countryside below, I marvelled at the power I possessed as I flew through the night sky – adorned with stars and a crescent moon.

On other nights, our father's muffled swearing and angry words would wake me as I lay in bed, uncertain and afraid of what might happen next. Sometimes, the tempest subsided and I would fall into an uneasy sleep.

On other occasions our mother sought refuge in our bedroom. At the time I had no idea why but, years later I realised, like many women, she was threatened by a husband's unwanted demands.

Most times, Gordon and I would sleep head to toe, leaving mum a bed of her own. There were also times when she lay next to me and I felt her body's warmth and listened to her breathing.

At first, I believed my mother when she said the bruises on her face were accidental. As more bruises appeared and as their arguing became more frequent, I realised she was hiding the truth.

Their relationship grew bitter and more violent. One

episode, like a scene of out of an old black and white *Keystone Cops* skit, saw mum wielding a knife and chasing dad up the road as he drove the old Ford Prefect. He would stop every 20 or so yards, let her get close and then drive off again. I think it was Spike Milligan who said that comedy and tragedy are two sides of the same mask.

As children, my brother and I watched our family fall apart and we knew that our parents no longer loved one another. Our father and mother drank to excess, the rent was in arrears and it was only because of Gordon and my part time work after school at the local milk bar that there was food on the table.

Our father spent days and nights in bed, a flagon of sherry by his side. His face took on the gaunt, haunted look of one possessed by demons and his health deteriorated so rapidly that he would sometimes fall to the floor, convulsing in an alcohol-induced, epileptic fit.

Looking at their wedding photo, all these years afterwards, I marvel at their faces, so full of youthful expectation and optimism, and wonder if the path had already been laid out that would lead to the despair and pain that would end their marriage.

As to what caused his descent into such an abyss, I'll never know. As a child I remember overhearing a story about dad losing his job as a suburban train driver after being held responsible for accidently killing someone at a pedestrian crossing.

I was also told that the reason we moved from St Kilda to Broadmeadows so many years before was because of a house fire where our family lost everything and our father was badly burnt.

During the off-season at the local football club, I spent a couple of months learning how to box. As I trained, little did I know to what end I was to put my new skill. Weeks later, when my father ignored a warning not to lay hands on mum, I knocked him to the floor.

As an adult, when recounting the story to other men, they sometimes tell me they wish they had done the same thing to their violent fathers. Does coming of age for a boy necessitate proving he is better than his father and that he can shelter and protect his mother?

Soon after, dad deserted the family and the three of us moved from Broadmeadows to a rented room in South Melbourne as the rent was in arrears and we were about to be evicted. Our reprieve only lasted a couple of months as it soon become obvious that our mother was incapable of looking after herself or taking responsibility for the two of us.

Like dad, she had turned to alcohol to try and erase the pain and torment she felt – only to find things spiralling out of control.

Torn between my allegiance to my mother and the possibility of embracing a better life, I'll never forget the day, as a 15 year old, I looked to the heavens, rejected my mother and prayed to God that she would not claim me so that I would be free to escape the past and begin anew.

Rescue came in the form of Mr Mackie from Broadmeadows High who gave Gordon and me temporary shelter in his home and made sure that we could continue at school by helping the two of us enrol at Melbourne High. As luck would have it, the task was helped by the fact that living in South Melbourne meant we were in the school's enrolment zone.

Part 4

A Fresh Beginning:
Melbourne High and a New Home

Melbourne High was, and still is, a selective boys school with strong academic standards and a reputation for discipline, hard work and a commitment to learning. The very things Gordon and I needed and acknowledged as the best way to have any chance of achieving a better life.

More like an independent, non-government school, at Melbourne High the teachers wore academic gowns at assembly, cadets paraded after school and boys made sure shoes were polished, shirt sleaves rolled down and buttoned and their hair was the regulation length.

During the 60s and 70s very few students in government schools, compared to current numbers, stayed on to years 11 and 12 and Melbourne High was unusual in that the expectation was that all students were destined for university.

After our years of violence, family arguments and uncertainty, the school provided a comforting, predictable and reassuring environment. I'll always remember being taken to Henry Buck's Menswear in the city to collect my business-like grey suit, shirts and school tie and being told by the then Principal Mr Thompson that the school expected much of us and that the challenge was there to be taken.

While they most likely knew of our past, none of the teachers talked about what we had experienced or tried to help us with counselling.

For better of for worse, this was a time before the self-esteem movement and the care, share grow approach to emotional well being and the expectation was to apply oneself, study hard and gain as much as possible from what was being offered.

Australian History, with Ben Munday, was entertaining, academically rigorous and unpredictable. When Mr Munday approached in the classroom one never knew whether he was about to throw your failed essay out the window, order you to get a haircut at the local barber shop or ask you to pick up some recently ordered cigars. On a number of occasions I was privileged to be asked to do the last of the three.

His classes, instead of being regimented and didactic were more like tutorials where, after the year's syllabus was outlined, over the course of the year students presented research papers and faced a barrage of questions.

Similar to what was expected at university we were taught to do our own research, both primary and secondary sources, and test assumptions and conclusions against the available evidence.

Unlike today, where students surf the world-wide-web or get tutors to write their essays over the internet, all our work was done in the school's library with an old fashioned Dewey Decimal system and row after row of well-read, earmarked books. Hours and hours were spent summarising arguments, making notes longhand and grappling with complex ideas and competing arguments.

Not surprisingly, given my background and parents' ancestry, my favourite topic in Australian History involved

Russell Ward's *The Australian Legend* and learning about romanticised stereotypes like the early convicts, bushrangers, the soldiers at Gallipoli and the young heroes of the Kokoda Track.

Mr Niven, the literature teacher, was also theatrical and to hear him recite Chaucer or a Shakespearean soliloquy was to be transported to the stage and to appreciate how language can sing with a musical quality.

While achieving a reasonable Year 12 result, the one blemish was failing Economics. A subject taught by Mr Drohan, who in addition to co-authoring the main textbook, went on to become the school principal after I had long left the school.

Although we had grown up in Broadmeadows with working-class parents, we never felt out of place. Students attended Melbourne High not because their parents could pay school fees or because they were from affluent homes but because of intelligence, ability and motivation.

Many of the teachers had grown up during the 30s Depression and survived the war. As a result, they had a down-to-earth, tempered quality that spoke of an egalitarian ethos – one that valued learning and the need for application if one was to succeed.

I subsequently found out that some of the teachers also lectured and tutored part time at the then Melbourne State College – long before it was forced to amalgamate with The University of Melbourne's Faculty of Education and theory overtook practical experience as the keystone when training teachers.

While at Melbourne High, with the financial support of some past students who were now successful businessmen calling themselves 'The Pups', we boarded with Mrs Edwards in Rosanna. A practical, generous woman from country NSW she fed, sheltered and treated us like her own.

Visiting the home of one of the old boys who lived in Toorak I was amazed to experience ducted heating for the first time and to take a ride in his Rolls Royce – a far cry from working-class Broadmeadows, our tired Housing Commission house and dad's clapped out Ford Prefect.

Like many baby boomers I look back on the late 60s and 70s as a turbulent time of social change and dislocation. Vietnam moratoriums, Woodstock and the rise of a youth culture advocating alternative life styles and overthrowing the status quo.

As students we were not immune. While in Year 12, along with a couple of other like-minded friends, I joined the Secondary Students for Secondary Action and imbibed the left's radical agenda.

Time was spent listening to protest songs by Peter, Paul and Mary, Joan Baez and Bob Dylan, as well as wagging school to join a discussion group led by Monash University's radical activist, Harry Van Moorst.

Like many other young people, intoxicated with the rebellious spirit of the time, we railed against American imperialism, the war against Communism and preached disarmament and world peace.

No one on the cultural left bothered to tell us about Stalin's purges where millions were killed or the fact that Mao's cultural revolution led to widespread famine, poverty, death and disease.

Part 5

University, Marriage and a Career

Not having any parents or resources of my own, the only reason university was a possibility was because I gained a studentship – a scheme whereby the Victorian Education Department paid fees and a living allowance on the condition that those signing up were willing to teach for at least three years after graduation.

Gordon had proven more successful in his Year 12 year and was fortunate enough to have gained a Commonwealth Scholarship to university. While dad had spoken of the university of life and referred to Melbourne's Pentridge Prison as the bluestone college, like many of our generation, Gordon and I were the first in our family to go to university.

The path to learning, though, was not without its challenges and bumps.

At the time of the French Revolution, Wordsworth wrote, "Bliss was it in that dawn to be alive, but to be young was very heaven". When I arrived at La Trobe University at the start of 1970 little did I realise that we were about to experience our very own revolution.

The counter culture movement was spreading from San Francisco's Haight-Ashbury, the message of 'make love not war' was the order of the day and marijuana and LSD were the drugs of preference.

Add the sexual revolution fuelled by the pill and Germaine Greer's *The Female Eunuch* and it is no wonder that many students dropped out – both metaphorically and literally.

This was a time when old certainties and truths were questioned and undermined. The cultural left reigned supreme and I'll always remember one of the more colourful slogans of the day – 'land rights for gay whales'.

I'll also remember the protests against conscription and the Vietnam War and the growing belief that institutions like marriage, the Church and Western civilisation were obsolete and guilty of reinforcing privilege and antiquated ideas about God and country.

My time as an undergraduate, to say the least, was less than impressive. Possibly, because of a broken home and violent parents, I lacked the discipline to work hard and apply myself.

The highlights of the week included hockey training and Saturday matches, cashing the studentship cheque and starting early at the local pub, the Summerhill, where we debated politics, current events and important existential questions like: 'Whose is the next shout?'

Another important event, one that has shaped a life-long enjoyment and love of overseas travel, was visiting a girlfriend whose father was stationed in Islamabad, Pakistan. This was a time when increasing numbers of hippies were on the overland trail from Australia to Europe and beyond and the Beatles had recently discovered Transcendental Meditation (TM) and the Maharishi Mahesh Yogi.

Like Spike Milligan, who had grown up in India living in an army barracks, I found the exotic sights, colours and sounds captivating. I still remember falling asleep on the overnight train from Madras to Delhi to the rhythmic, regular sounds of wheels against track and waking to the early morning shouts of 'chai, chai' at dimly lit, crowded stations engulfed by noise and steam.

Driving through the Khyber Pass to Kabul, and hearing about what had happened to the British in the first Afghan war in 1839, I now appreciate why that country can never be conquered and why armies from Russia, America, Australia and other allied nations have found the task so elusive and difficult.

Returning to La Trobe, after the trip to India and Afghanistan and after spending time at the same ashram where the Beatles had discovered TM, I proved to be a popular character. Wearing a tribal Afghan coat, sandalwood beads that had been dipped in the Ganges and recounting stories of universal peace and harmony, made me very much a child of the times.

Failing a year and having to show cause why I should be allowed to re-enrol provided a reality check. Meeting and going out with Julia, a fellow La Trobe student, also focused my mind and made me realise that future happiness and prosperity relied on knuckling down and getting serious.

Deciding that Julia was the chosen one was, I have to admit, an easy decision. She had an innocence and zest for life that was infectious and offered the stability and assurance that I lacked.

Better still, not only did she drive an Austin A40 soft top, she also volunteered to drive me to the local pub and she was, and still is, an excellent cook. In this post-modern, feminist age the saying 'the best way to a man's heart is through his stomach' appears chauvinistic but, back then, it contained more than an element of truth.

Julia, when less than a year old, and her family had arrived as ten-pound poms after the war to escape the destruction and hardship of post-war London. The family had first moved to country Mildura where Eileen, Julia's mother, had to confront goannas, a wood-fired stove, 100 degree heat and sayings like 'g'day mate' and 'I hope the kids aren't crook'.

Her dad was a motor mechanic and after spending years travelling around country Victoria they finally settled in Melbourne where Julia attended Kew High School. As often happens, Julia, being creative, wanted to enrol in Graphic Design at RMIT after Year 12 but, instead, had to take up the offer of an Economics Degree at La Trobe University.

We were married in 1974 and this was the year I most enjoyed and did best at in terms of academic results. Julia was teaching at Eltham High and our first home was a small unit in Upper Heidelberg Road, Ivanhoe.

Like many newlyweds, we did it hard – Julia's parents donated a second-hand fridge, the mattress was on the floor and the only bookshelf was made of second-hand bricks and wooden planks. But, for me, the opportunity provided a new and better life and, at last, the chance to find happiness and to share life with a loved one.

Melbourne was very different then. Colour TV had only been recently introduced, there were no mobile phones or internet, formal dinner parties were all the rage and wines called Mateus Rose and Cold Duck were fashionable.

Cookbooks by Robert Carrier, Margaret Fulton and the Presbyterian Women's Association were popular and nobody had heard of nouvelle cuisine or recipes from the pacific rim – although, we did have a copy of *The Complete Asian Cookbook* by Charmaine Solomon.

One of the first expensive dinners we could afford remains

a highlight – this was a time when men had to wear a shirt and jacket, women dressed accordingly and dishes such as French onion soup, a rack of lamb, peppered steak, crème brulee and lemon soufflé were considered sophisticated.

After years where anyone who drank wine was in danger of being called a plonko, now was the time when post-war migrants from Italy and Greece taught us about the pleasures of good wine and the need for families to civilise their children by taking them out to dinner and teaching them table manners.

I started teaching in 1975 in a western suburban school in a migrant community where many of the parents spoke little English. I enjoyed being among young people and offering them what education had provided for me – the chance to learn and the chance to experience a better life.

Maybe as a result of being idealistic, we all felt teaching was a profession imbued with the desire to help others. Also, because of my working-class background and the fact it was only because of a studentship that I was able to go to university, I felt that being a teacher was a privilege and that the obligation was to help others.

It also shouldn't surprise as dad was an alcoholic and a poor father that while at Broadmeadows High and Melbourne High I looked to the teachers I admired as examples to follow. Boys need strong male role models to guide and mentor them.

Broadmeadows was a distant memory as I threw myself into teaching. Over the 18 years that I taught, at Merrilands High, St Helena Post Primary and, finally, at Camberwell Grammar School, I strove to do my best and to excite students' imagination and love for literature, to help them master the structure of an English sentence and to teach them how to write a well crafted, lucid essay.

Marking Year 12 English papers, being on the Panel of Examiners and various state-wide committees kept me busy and provided the stimulation, satisfaction and recognition I needed after a dislocated childhood so full of despair.

After teaching for a number of years I also realised, if I was to progress, that I needed to keep up-to-date. So I enrolled back at La Trobe where I ended up completing a Master of Education and Doctor of Philosophy in curriculum studies.

Like many newlyweds, we had our ups and downs. I was sometimes guilty of taking our relationship for granted, but as with any successful marriage we learned to compromise, to respect one another's needs and to enjoy our time together.

When we had arguments, possibly because of memories of my parents' bitter and violent fights, instead of being confrontational I would jump in the car and drive – not returning until hours later after my temper had cooled.

Travelling to Europe over the Christmas break one year and being forced to live and travel so close together cemented the marriage as the trip gave us the time to better understand and appreciate one another.

Julia introduced me to great sculpture and art: from Michelangelo's 'David' and Botticelli's 'Birth of Venus' to Monet's 'Water Lilies' and the works of Matisse. Like many before us and many yet to come we stared in awe at the Acropolis, walked the narrow, old world streets of the Marais and stood expectedly waiting for Big Ben to chime the hour.

As any traveller can tell you, though, when arriving in a strange, foreign city not everything works out to plan. On arriving in Paris late one night, I had mistakenly booked a room in a hotel situated in the red light area and we were kept awake for most of the night by the sounds of the working girls and their customers. We kept our clothes on and slept on top of the blanket and sheets, departing early the next morning.

A few days later, on seeing the white cliffs of Dover from the deck of the Channel ferry, our spirits were lifted realising that we would soon be in England. Julia had relatives there and, for me, the excitement was to finally arrive and breathe the air of the land made so memorable by Shakespeare, Austen, Dickens and T. S. Eliot.

Even though my ancestry was Irish Catholic, and my grandmother had told me of the terror and brutality of the Black and Tans, the history I had been taught and the literature I valued and loved spoke of England.

On returning to Melbourne and teaching we began to think it was time to start a family. Julia had always said that she would have our first child before she turned 30 and that is what happened. James was born when Julia was 29 and his birth, while a harrowing experience for Julia, for me, was one of the highlights of my life.

The birth of our daughter Amelia three years later was equally as memorable but, at the same time, different. Is it something primordial that gives men so much pleasure in gaining a son?

For me, especially given my family history, becoming a father was more life changing than getting married and life was never to be the same. The added responsibility of having children made me realise that I had to succeed and provide a childhood for James and Amelia that I had never been able to experience.

Fortunately, Julia had the luxury now denied to so many women of being a full-time mother. After the initial chaos of sleepless nights, early morning feeds and broken routines we soon became accustomed to being parents.

Not that a teacher's salary provided an extravagant lifestyle; while at home Julia built children's art and craft boxes, moulded clay garden-birds and occasionally worked as a waitress to help make ends meet.

Winston Churchill, either rightly or wrongly, is attributed with the expression: "If a man is not a socialist by the time he is 20, he has no heart. If he is not a conservative by the time he is 40, he has no brain."

Such was my experience. The teenage years as a member of the Eureka Youth Movement, the time at university being involved in anti-war protests and my experience as a branch president for the militant Victorian Secondary Teachers Association, like my father, proved that I had a passion for change and for challenging the status quo.

As I grew older, though, and after finding out about how many had suffered and died because of Western appeasement to Communist dictators including Stalin, Mao, Pol Pot and Ho Chi Minh, I began to question cultural-left ideology and causes.

In response to the argument that meritocracy and competition in education were unacceptable, and that learning had to focus on the future and not the past, I also found myself becoming more conservative.

For me, being a father also dramatically changed my perspective of life and I redoubled my efforts to build a career and to provide for the four of us. In addition to teaching, I started writing on education for the print media, especially for *The Australian*, and also became active in the Liberal Party.

One option, that never eventuated, was to gain pre-selection and enter parliament. The other option, that did happen, was to leave teaching and start an education consulting business. Firstly, with Education Strategies and then the Education Standards Institute I specialised in curriculum work, both in Australia and overseas, and also published a number of books.

Better still, I became heavily involved in the public debate on education and, while not liked by the education establishment, gained a reputation as one of Australia's more vocal conservative education authors and commentators.

Being a consultant not only provided a rewarding and stimulating career, it also meant, while not financially well off, that I was able to give Julia, James and Amelia a comfortable, enjoyable lifestyle.

In many ways, our marriage and way of life mirrored John Howard's ideal of a suburban, middle class family – a house with a picket fence in a comfortable suburb, children at independent schools and the occasional vacation in Port Douglas or Noosa.

For me, marriage, children and a profession epitomised everything that I most struggled to achieve in life and I finally felt, unlike my parents, that all was well. Little did I realise what was to come, and like a Greek tragedy, how the gods were about to turn my world upside down and destroy what was most precious in life.

Part 6

Bastille Day
The Day of the Accident

I had only seen death once. It was an accident where a car had run off the road returning from a day's skiing at Mt Bulla and I was asked to help lift a body from the wreckage. The thing that surprised me most was how heavy and inert the body was and how I remained so calm and detached.

In many ways we have become desensitised to death. We see carnage and destruction regularly on the nightly news and read about it in the daily press. Ours is a society where materialism dominates and the promise is of eternal youth and physical comfort.

The second time was different. Looking at the face of James, my dead son, as he lay seemingly asleep and covered in a white hospital sheet struck me to the core with an aching sense of bewilderment and loss.

Still in a state of shock and disbelief, the words "vanity of vanities; all is vanity" came to mind as I clutched my wife's hand. To remember words from the Bible was unexpected, while raised as a Catholic, I did not attend church as often as I should.

Years of parenting, years of watching over and reading bedtime stories, holidays, birthdays, Saturday sport, learning the clarinet and university – all to no avail and destroyed without reason.

As I gazed at his face, half listening, I heard my daughter Amelia recite: "Good night sweet prince, and flights of angels sing thee to thy rest." Strange, how in times of suffering and distress we turn to half remembered truths and lessons from the past.

From our unconscious, fragments of songs, poems and lines memorised long ago while at school bubble to the surface and resonate with a profound and immediate sense of meaning.

As if in a dream, I followed the nurse into the next room to sign a paper affirming the identity of James. I remember signing the form but have no idea what was written. It no longer mattered.

Earlier that morning we had been awakened by a loud and unexpected knock on our front door. Seeing two police, I thought that James had got into a fight or been involved in some stupid prank.

Only weeks before, he had suffered from what his mates called a UDI, an unintended drunken incident, and he required a trip to hospital and a couple of stiches. Accompanied by Amelia, I had taken him to the same hospital in which he now lay. I remember watching the nurse stitch his cut and thinking, for all his bravado and manly strength, how vulnerable he was and how deeply I loved him.

Was this a premonition heralding what was to follow? Were events already in motion and like a Greek tragedy, had the gods already decided that James would suffer a far worse injury the next time there was an accident?

As I stood with the two police, Julia and Amelia rushed into the lounge room to hear the words, 'Your son has been killed in a hit and run accident'. I wonder now, did the two police stop by the front gate to decide who was to deliver the news. Did they debate the best way to tell us? Should we be asked to sit down, should we be given time to dress?

No matter, as they say, death waits for no one and they were direct and to the point. When in shock, reality distorts and time takes on a life of its own. As I watched, Julia, as in slow motion, walked across the room to raise the curtain. In doing something so mundane and routine, did she hope that life would continue as normal?

The first day of James' death passed in a procession of phone calls, flowers delivered, relatives and friends offering tears and embraces and questions seeking answers about what had happened and why.

The first people to be told of James' death where our close friends and neighbours who lived two streets away, Vic and Judy. Did I walk or did I drive? I cannot remember. What I do remember is their stunned look of bewilderment and anguish.

Telling family members, for me, was easy. Both parents had long since died and my brother, Gordon, lived in Minnesota – I decided to phone him later in the day, early morning stateside.

Julia's family were next and throughout the morning Julia phoned them. Sylvia, my sister in law, after running restaurants was now a celebrant, and she quickly arrived and took control of events.

Sylvia was to be a blessing, sleeping on the couch for the next few nights, answering the phone, greeting visitors and neighbours at the door and helping to organise the funeral held later that week.

Julia's brother and his wife, Chris and Carol were at their farm in the Otways and their children were scattered across the globe – Bali, Spain, Italy and Ireland. So distant, but bonded to James with love and shared childhood memories. I still wonder what it must have been like for each of them.

Flying back to Melbourne, a long flight surrounded by other travellers who knew nothing of their cousin's death. How did they cope and make sense of what was happening? Did they fill the time watching movies, try and catch a few hours sleep, or like us, feel that time was out of joint and the world turned upside down.

The thing I most remember when they all arrived is that very few words were spoken. This was a time of embraces and sobbing as death had torn away the veneer of composure and reduced us all to what is elemental and tribal.

It was as though the house had become magnet, attracting unconditional love, sympathy and support. The smell of perfumed flowers filled the air, relatives and friends arrived unannounced with offerings of food and neighbours helped with the daily chores.

Nothing will erase the memory of the look on Julia's girlfriends' faces as they arrived at the house with casseroles, legs of ham and other supplies. Only women who have suffered the pains of childbirth and suckled a new-born infant can fully appreciate the depths of despair that every mother feels on losing a child.

For me, the imperative was to go to the scene of the accident. What did I hope to achieve? I knew that nothing could be changed, time would not unwind but, there was an urge to stand where he had last been alive and to try and understand what had happened.

Was it fate and who was to blame? Did James suffer and was there a chance he could have been saved? Uninvited, Shakespeare's lines came into my mind, "As flies to wanton boys are we to the gods. They kill us for their sport."

It was a short drive as James was hit only a few kilometres from where we lived – a short walk from the safety of home. Even though it was still early morning and the accident had occurred only hours earlier, the word had got around. A group of mates stood and sat, each with a look of utter despondency and despair.

Someone had placed flowers where his lifeless body had been found by two friends returning from the same party where, only hours before, they had shared jokes, laughed and danced the night away. A school blazer lay nearby and cards and pictures completed the scene.

Many of those who had gathered had been to school with James and as I looked in each face, I felt their incomprehension and sadness reach out to me. Inconsolable grief washed over us as we stood helpless, unable to comprehend or change what had happened.

Over the next few years, a loving bond born out of mutual suffering and time with James would bind Julia, Amelia and me to his friends as they provided companionship in what were to be the most difficult and painful years of our lives.

Looking at the accident scene, it was impossible to tell what had happened. The only thing we knew was that James, with a friend, was walking home from a party and earlier that morning he had been struck by a car driving along Canterbury Road. His friend, just before the accident, had turned left at Monomeath Avenue, with James continuing alone on his journey home.

The driver did not stop and the police had no idea what type of vehicle it was or who had been driving. Over the next two years, the pieces of the puzzle were put together as the police identified the car involved, the driver responsible and gathered enough evidence through wiretaps and examining the car to take the matter to court.

The nightmare that was 14th July, Bastille Day, ended with the three of us being driven to the morgue. What good would it do and what did we hope to achieve, I do not know. A parent's instinct is strong and a child's presence is imprinted in his or her very being – possibly one last chance to see our son and to wish him farewell.

They refused to let us near James and I could only see his body dimly through a darkened window. I remember little else of that first night, except for drinking too much, breaking a glass and crying in a drunken rage. Why me? What had I done wrong? Why hadn't I been there to save him?

Around and around in my head ran the line: "Those whom the gods wish to destroy, they first make mad."

Strange, how life and death are so inextricably linked but while we respond to the first with hope and optimism with death most of us are in the dark. The rituals are unknown or forgotten and as we discovered, there are no guideline to follow.

I remember reading that in Victorian England, bereaved ones would wear black, pictures of the departed would be draped and the time for grieving was set. Julia, Amelia and I did not have the same certainty as we embarked on a storm tossed, bewildering journey that would test and challenge each one of us and our love for one another.

Part 7

Ground Zero

In my diary for 14th July 2002, I've written 'ground zero'. I'll always remember James waking us as the World Trade Centre was destroyed in the terrorist attack of September 11, 2001. Little did I realise then that like those families who suffered, we were to face our own time of death and loss.

It's only now, looking back, that I realise how profoundly affected I was by James' death. I couldn't face the local shopkeepers and their looks of concern and pain, so I shopped elsewhere.

When I left the house I wore sunglasses, wanting to shield people from my eyes and what they would reveal. During the long nights of troubled and broken sleep, I kept repeating Kurtz's cry from the *Heart of Darkness*, "The horror! The horror!"

During waking hours, for no apparent reason or because of memories of our time together, like a child, I would break into uncontrollable sobbing.

Every time I walked across a road, I thought of James' death and when driving became impatient and reckless.

Even now, when in a social situation and somebody asks, 'how many children do you have?' I feel uncertain about what to reply. Should I admit that James is dead and open the wound and suffer a look of embarrassment and pain or take the easy option and say he never existed?

Having been an English teacher for so many years, it was only natural that literature would play such a significant role in attempting to deal with what had happened and what was to come. In that first week, I kept thinking of the lines from Yeats' *The Second Coming* that I had studied so many years earlier:

> *Things fall apart; the centre cannot hold;*
> *Mere anarchy is loosed upon the world,*

My world, without warning or reason, suddenly fell apart as what I most cherished in life was stolen. It was ironic that the very thing I was denied as a child and had successfully built as James was growing up – a secure and happy family – was now lost.

As parents, so much of what we do and think is based on the assumption that our children will always be safe and secure and that we will die before them. The natural order of events is full of life and promise, otherwise why bother? If we opened ourselves to the futility of life, all would be bleak and devoid of meaning. Our daily lives would be insufferable.

I was numbed by shock and without the sympathy and support of family and friends and Julia's unremitting love and Amelia's presence the sense of loss would have been unbearable.

There was also the start of the police investigation into the hit and run accident to keep the three of us occupied. Like an incident from CSI, the police had gathered shards of the car's front indicator cover from the accident scene. On gluing it together, they were able to identify the type of vehicle from the part number.

They knew that James had been hit by a Nissan Navara, the only problem was that there were hundreds of models registered in Victoria and they faced the prospect of having to inspect every one.

The accident had received widespread media coverage, including interviews and TV appearances to call on the public to help the police catch the driver. For me, the pain of loss was mixed with the need for revenge, to identify who had killed James and to see whoever it was brought to justice.

James' death was made so much worse as we didn't know what had happened and who was responsible. In the days after the accident I drove over the same route that he had taken from the party, again and again, trying to picture the scene and work out why the driver had not veered to avoid hitting James or braked in time.

For Julia there was the heartbreaking knowledge that her son had been hit and left by the side of the road to die – as she said, something you would not do to a dog. Raised to abide by the law and to do justice to others, we were shattered to think that somebody could be so cruel and inhuman as to not stop and render assistance.

Except for when she has no other choice, Julia still refuses to drive past the accident scene – a scene haunted with the inescapable reality of her son's death.

It was not until the case was heard in March 2005 that the driver responsible finally pleaded guilty to failing to stop to help James and conspiring to hide his guilt – it would take a further two years and eight months after the hit and run accident before we would have a clearer picture of what had happened to our son.

Each night, Julia and I fell into bed, emotionally and physically exhausted. We slept fitfully and in the early hours, at the time we imagine James had been hit, we woke to what seemed an empty and cold house.

Listening to the winter wind howling through the trees and the rain beating against the window, I relived the fear and pain I experienced as a child when my mother and father fought – swearing at one another, with my father in a drunken rage.

I felt the warmth of Julia next to me and held on to her, seeking refuge against the emptiness and reassurance that all would be well.

In the morning, I quietly opened the door to Amelia's room to see her huddled under her doona. Listening to her breathing, I prayed that she would survive the trauma of her brother's death and that she would find the understanding and strength to make sense of what had happened.

In a secular age, while it might surprise, it is understandable why so many of us return to the church and its rituals in times of need and in times of celebration – baptisms, marriages and funerals.

This life is transitory and there is a limit to our ability to comprehend events. While science has split the atom and put a man on the moon, when it comes to tragedy and untimely death, there is a human urge to look more deeply and to find solace in something more lasting and profound than our day-to-day, worldly existence.

There is a need to recognise that each of us has a soul and that our flesh and blood existence represents only one aspect of who we are and what we have the potential to become.

Standing beside James' open coffin in the funeral parlour, a couple of days before the church service, was confronting. In many ways, the experience was surreal – Julia had been asked to dress James and as I stood there, for no reason, I wondered why she provided shoes and his best clothes? Why, if they were to be burnt when the coffin was cremated.

When walking outside to the car Julia commented that it was like looking at an empty shell. Whatever was most precious and life giving in James had departed and all that was left was a lifeless body that once was our son and a brother to Amelia.

The funeral service was held on 20th July, at St Mark's Church.

During the years I taught at James' school and joined in to sing hymns like *Be Thou My Vision* and *I Vow To Thee My Country*, little did I realise that both would be sung at my son's funeral. The lines from T. S. Eliot's *Little Gidding V* also featured in the service:

> *And all shall be well and*
> *All manner of thing shall be well*

It was only later that I found out that the Christian mystic, Julian of Norwich – much earlier than Eliot – had used the same words to express her conviction, in a world of suffering, uncertainty and pain, that there is hope and solace in giving one's self up to God.

The service, described as a celebration, was physically and emotionally draining, but at the same time, uplifting. Being surrounded by family and friends, especially James' mates, made me realise how much James was loved and how many others were also suffering and sharing our pain.

Gathering in the church where James had sung in the school's Christmas choir service, seeing over 500 family, friends, and many whose names I did not know united in memory of our son was comforting.

During his 20 years, he touched many lives and left a profound and moving sense of companionship, laughter and love. James' uncle Chris summed it up so well when he said in his eulogy:

> *We remember an incredibly genuine young man with a great zest for life; a slightly quirky charmer who had a large circle of friends, both male and female, who loved him dearly. Why not? He was a deeply loyal, caring, dependable and uncomplicated fellow.*
>
> *One of James' teachers wrote to Julia and Kevin describing him as a person who infected everyone around him with his personal magic. Another spoke of him as a person who made others feel good. In the large Donnelly family photo album James can be seen grinning or laughing in virtually every photo – that cheeky, slightly enigmatic, knowing grin that he wore so much of the time.*

That night, after the formal wake, family and friends came back to the house. The night passed in a blur of music, drinks, food and conversation. What was said, I cannot remember. I know that it rained and that early the next morning I lay awake listening to the wind swirling around the house. Was it James' spirit returning home for the last time, to let us know that he was free and that we should not grieve?

During that first week and in the following months, we all experienced signs of James' presence. One night the light outside James' bedroom appeared to turn on by itself and on another night Amelia awoke, sensing that her brother was sitting at the end of her bed, watching over her.

Years later when Amelia and I were in London, on the first day of the trip, for no reason, we jumped off the bus halfway along Fleet Street to be confronted by a sign in front of a coffee shop saying *Jamies*. Soon after, crossing the street and heading to St Paul's Cathedral, we happened to look in the window of a restaurant to see a wall covered by a reproduction of a work by Matisse titled *The King's Sadness*.

We have a copy of an original lithograph on our wall at home. It depicts a drummer, guitarist and dancer and given its vibrancy, colour, movement and musical motif it didn't surprise that James loved it so much.

What led us to travel half way around the world to be confronted with memories of a lost son and brother? Is it possible that loved ones beyond the grave reach back into this life or is it because we are so heartbroken that we yearn for renewed contact?

I'll never know the answer. What I did realise the morning after the wake – as we spent the day cleaning the house, washing glasses and dishes, discarding old flowers and taking the empty bottles to the tip – was that the three of us were now alone. With the funeral service complete, the next stage of our family's journey was set to begin.

Part of that journey was burying James' remains at a country property that he loved dearly and that had special significance to our family. Many of James' ex-school friends volunteered to be involved and over three days we prepared his burial place and cut a bush track from the house to where he was laid to rest.

The boys, in particular, threw themselves into the physical work and each night they ate and drank around the campfire, reminiscing about their time with James at school and their exploits while at university.

Contrary to the belief that boys cannot express sorrow or are uncomfortable with grief some of James' mates, including members of the bands Zoophtye and Spindrift, also produced a musical CD titled *Ode to J.D* where they sang of James and the impact of his death. They also organised a live concert where we all got together to share the love and affection for a son, brother and mate who also loved music.

The bond between all of us is a special one and the occasion provided a kind of ritual where we shared our pain and loss and drew on one another for comfort and support. Over the years since the hit and run accident many of the boys, some of whom I taught at Camberwell Grammar, have become like a second family – a family united by grief and the need to find comfort and reassurance in one another.

As one of the boy's wrote on the anniversary's of the hit and run accident:

Turn back the days
And take the precious time

I still see you walk into the room
On the smiles of everyone there

I feel you, warm in my heart
When I look at a friend across the table

We all know each others' thoughts
It is the understanding you left behind

You sit next to me so often
In a place thats ours forever

Where cobwebs will never hang
That nothing can ever fill

You condense us all
With the hardest bond

But you've released to me
A love I did not know

I'd like to believe that in being so open to one another, sharing the pain and loss and keeping in touch, the boys have helped one another, and us, to keep the black dog at bay.

Part 8

Left Alone

In the week following James' death the house was full of friends and family and I was buoyed and comforted by their love, sympathy and willingness to share our suffering and pain.

That time was gone and the three of us were now alone. After the drama of the hit and run accident, the hectic coming and going of family and friends and the build up to the church service, there was an anti-climax.

On the day of the funeral somebody, I forget who, told me that families who suffered tragedies like ours often fell apart under the weight of their anguish and loss. I prayed that such would not be our fate.

For days I had survived on adrenaline and the need to organise James' funeral and to present a brave face on the day. I now felt exhausted, empty and overwhelmed by the futility of life. Never before had the words of Macbeth's soliloquy sounded so true:

> *Tomorrow, and tomorrow, and tomorrow,*
> *Creeps in this petty pace from day to day,*
> *To the last syllable of recorded time;*
> *And all our yesterdays have lighted fools*
> *The way to dusty death. Out, out, brief candle!*
> *Life's but a walking shadow, a poor player,*

That struts and frets his hour upon the stage,
And then is heard no more. It is a tale
Told by an idiot, full of sound and fury,
Signifying nothing.

For some years I had worked for myself after establishing an education consulting business. I had also written for the newspapers on education and enjoyed being involved in politics and public debate.

All was premised on safeguarding and providing for the family and now that one of the closest things to my heart had been torn away, life seemed worthless and without value. Is it misguided manly pride or some deep seated biological necessity that forces fathers to play the role of protector and guardian?

Whatever the reason, losing a son strikes at the very core of your being and nothing remains as it was. A line from Yeats' *Easter 1916* kept running through my mind, "All is changed, changed utterly."

In the weeks and months after the funeral, every day, there were reminders of what had happened and the inescapable reality that our son and Amelia's brother was no longer with us. For years, as a family we had shared dinner, now the chair where James once sat entertaining us with his experiences at university or what he and his mates had been up to the night before was empty.

Closing James' bank account, notifying Monash University of what had happened and cancelling his mobile phone reinforced the fact that all he had hoped and planned to achieve were no more. Worse still, as a father I would never share the milestones that parents expect to share with their sons and daughters – a 21st birthday, career and, hopefully, a wedding and grandchildren.

His room was silent and Julia and I had to decide what to do with his belongings. Some people create a shrine for their dead son or daughter, we did not. Gradually, we cleared his desk, removed his clothes and a pile of textbooks and notes.

Julia suggested we offer some of his better jackets and hoodies to his close mates as keep sakes but I quickly said no. I'm sure that it would have been too hard for them and, to be frank, it was also too hard for me to think that somebody might be walking around in his clothes.

One day, I discovered his clarinet case and debated whether I should open it or not. James had studied the clarinet during his school years and one of our proudest moments was to hear him play Mozart's Clarinet Concerto as part of his Year 12 music examination.

As I held his case in my hands, I remembered all those times he complained about having to practice and how I used to enjoy watching his agile fingers dancing along the instrument. Years after the accident, I came across a VHS tape of his practice music examination – I could only bare watching for a few seconds as he magically translated notes on a page into vibrations in the air that touched the soul.

As the police had not, as yet, identified the driver who had hit James, there were also the incessant doubts and questions about what had happened early that morning and whether the guilty driver would be caught and punished. For those parents who lose a child whose body is never found and who never discover what happened, I can only begin to imagine the suffering and pain experienced.

At least for us, even though it took over two years before the driver was convicted and sentenced and we had to suffer the trauma of reliving that day in a number of court cases, we eventually saw the guilty punished and had a clearer idea of what had happened that night.

The Monday after the funeral Amelia returned to school. Watching her struggle through the remaining months of Year 12, dazed and numbed by the experience, also tore at my heart. James was Amelia's cherished older brother, mentor and someone in whom she could confide. While growing up the two had been inseparable and shared a love of music, Nando's, discussing life's mysteries and what the future might hold.

Amelia's speech at the funeral was outstanding. Surrounded by a group of James' mates she spoke in an assured, clear and moving voice, as though possessed by a higher force. Of James, she said:

> *It has come as a deep and disturbing shock that a man passionate for life and 'living it up' has had his life stolen from him at the age of 20. It is hard to comprehend that James, who had so many prospects for the future, is no longer physically with us. But his incredible presence, that could light a gloomy room or 'get a party started' will be with us forever. James lived life like the flame of a fire – intense, free, unpredictable and he radiated heat that warmed everybody he met. I ask that in this painful time in all of your lives, that when you might be feeling cold or numb, that you let your fond memories of James burn as fierce and free as a fire, and let his spirit warm you from the tips of your fingers to the tips of your toes.*

Like Julia and I, Amelia was buoyed by the love and comfort of those around her and the need to acknowledge and celebrate her brother's life. At the same time, I could hardly look into her eyes as they revealed so much pain, suffering and incomprehension as to why her brother had been taken.

Amelia, years later, told me that she could not remember the second half of her Year 12 as she was running on automatic. The shock and loss blanketed her as she mechanically went through her daily routine. It would take another couple of years before the full extent of the damage caused by losing her brother erupted and we experienced yet another time of anxiety and disruption.

Seeing the impact on Julia of losing her son also cut me to the quick. Like every mother, Julia had anxiously watched over her child as he grew into a young man, happy and relieved that he had survived his adolescent years. To see him cut down so cruelly and senselessly only a few months before his 21st birthday broke her heart.

Watching her during the week after James' death I felt like a helpless child, powerless to make things right or to give the comfort and reassurance she needed. Outwardly, brave and resolute, Julia guarded what was left of her family and did everything she could to keep us together and to remain optimistic.

While I turned to literature in an effort to deal with what had happened, Julia relied on music and a heightened spiritual sense. After reading about the life of Julian of Norwich, *Revelations of Divine Love*, in her diary Julia quoted an extract:

> *Our faith is not merely a matter of being given*
> *suitably convincing arguments and reasons. We*

*sometimes have to learn to stay with the mystery,
to live the tension and bear the burden of our
pain. Healing is not instantaneous, nor is growth.
Julian had to learn to live through the tensions of
faith. So Julian reminds us that our experience of
God is not simply an academic, intellectual thing.
It is something that must be learnt through our
own pain and confusion. It is this pain and effort
that teaches us our own fragility and it is our
fragility that is the means God uses to teach us
about himself, his mercy, his healing power and
his creative purposes for us.*

Similar to Amelia, beneath Julia's composure and stoicism were churning anxieties, fears and a deep sense of loss. The pain was made worse by the fact that it took so long for the guilty driver to be identified and convicted for killing our son.

Even though the driver had left the scene, hid and repaired his damaged car, convinced his parents to lie about what had happened and perjured himself, the police were able to identify the car by rebuilding a shattered front indicator light cover.

The warning to spare parts suppliers to watch out for anyone ordering parts for the same make and model of the car paid off, as some months later, the driver had a second accident and the police were able to identify a suspect.

Months of secret wire taping and interviews followed, plus examining the damage to the car that was still evident, followed by a series of court cases involving the Magistrates Court, the County Court and Victoria's Supreme Court.

After denying his guilt, the driver at the final hour, pleaded guilty and was convicted of failing to stop, failing to render assistance and perverting the course of justice. Any thoughts that justice was finally to be done were shattered when the judge handed down a sentence of two years and three months – with a non-parole period of 10 months.

The realisation that the driver, instead of serving the full sentence, might be free in 10 months destroyed any faith we had in the justice system. The fact the non-parole period was extended to 18 months as a result of an appeal by the Director of Public Prosecutions did provide some sense of balance.

Any sense that we had been justified in arguing that the original non-parole period was 'manifestly inadequate' evaporated, though, on finding out some months later that the Adult Parole Board had placed the driver on home detention. Instead of serving the non-parole period of 18 months the driver would now enjoy the comforts of home after serving only 12 months.

So much for truth in sentencing and for the justice system ensuring that those guilty of committing a crime are properly punished. For our family, now destined to endure years of loss and distress, it appeared that the rights of the guilty outweighed the rights of those who were destined to suffer the most.

Part 9

Dealing with Loss

How we deal with depression caused by sorrow and loss is different for each one of us. While there are stages of grieving that might be common – shock, numbness, anger, denial, sorrow, resignation, acceptance and healing – how we deal with fate depends on our character, experience of life and the help and influence of those we love.

Death can also appear in many guises and circumstances. A mother or father dying in the fullness of time and being released from the illness and suffering of old age, while painful and distressing, is in many ways welcome.

The weekly news cycle involving thousands dying because of floods, famine, war, poverty and disease, while distressing and unfortunate, desensitises us to suffering, especially when the victims are far away and unnamed.

Closer to home, to lose a child without warning and while he or she is young, pierces every parent's heart with its injustice and cruelty.

James' death destroyed the family that Julia and I had spent years nurturing and protecting. For me, it also rekindled childhood fears and haunting memories that had lain dormant for years. Worst still, the very thing that I was denied as a child and that I had spent so long building, was now shattered.

Outwardly, like many men who suffer depression, I appeared to be coping and, as much as possible, I returned to a daily routine and did what was expected. The reality of running your own business is that if you do not work, there is no money. Fortunately, there were a couple of on-going education projects that would keep the wolf from the door.

One of the projects I worked on involved producing anti-smoking and anti-drug classroom materials across Australia, New Zealand and a number of countries in South East Asia and the Pacific. Once again, I was able to indulge myself with overseas travel.

Laos became a special place of escape and seclusion far from Melbourne and the everyday reminders of James' death. Watching the evening sun caress the slow, ever moving Mekong, listening to the laughter and shouts of children splashing water buffalo and lighting incense in dimly lit Buddhist temples provided solace.

Watching bent over farmers, plodding alongside shrines to their gods and ancestors, rhythmically planting rice by hand as they had done for hundreds of years, an eternal cycle of life beyond our comprehension and control, also comforted me.

Visiting Cambodia's killing fields and the infamous torture cells in Phnom Penh's Security Prison S-21 made me recognise the unimaginable horror and pain thousands of others have suffered, and continue to suffer, and to understand that we are not alone in our grief.

In the months and years following the hit and run accident I sought solace in keeping busy and maintaining a veneer of confidence and optimism. Putting on a suit and tie, meeting others in a work situation meant that the day went quickly and there was little opportunity or time to reflect or dwell on what had happened.

Beneath the surface, I was struggling and lost in a storm tossed sea, far from safety. The lines King Lear spoke after his daughter's death resonated again and again:

> *No, no, no life!*
> *Why should a dog, a horse, a rat, have life,*
> *And thou no breath at all? Thou'lt come no more,*
> *Never, never, never, never, never!*

I feared, like my father, that I was spiralling downwards into depression and turning to alcohol for forgetfulness. Like him, I became angry and short tempered, bursting into rage at the slightest provocation.

Emotionally, I felt vulnerable and defenceless and, increasingly, turned to Julia for support and comfort. The danger, as I knew, was that I relied on her too much and was draining her of the energy and strength she needed.

What kept me going?

I knew that as mortals, every one of us, at some stage or another, has to experience pain and sorrow. As a young boy growing up in Broadmeadows, I had experienced my fair share. I also believe that this world is caught between heaven and hell and, in the words of Alexander Pope, we are "Created half to rise, and half to fall".

While we like to believe that we control everything and that we can construct a perfect life, the reality is that to be human is to be vulnerable to loss and suffering. As a Catholic, there is also the belief that we have been expelled from the Garden of Eden and that utopia will never be found on this earth.

I remember once listening to what I later found out to be Bunyan's *The Pilgrim's Progress* on the radio – one of the expressions that stayed with me is "the slough of despond".

One of the Irish poet Yeats' poems refers to something similar when he talks about the "foul rag and bone shop of the heart". Both suggest that to be fully alive we need to acknowledge dark and light, despair as well as hope – you cannot experience one without the other.

As noted by another poet, William Blake: "Without Contraries is no progression. Attraction and Repulsion, Reason and Energy, Love and Hate, are necessary to Human existence."

Denial never addresses the issue and while burying a loss might bring temporary relief, the pain and suffering usually erupts later in depression and anger. Men, in particular, are prone to denying what is most destructive and presenting a façade where all appears to be well.

Far better, as women appear to know instinctively, is to honour your feelings and to acknowledge the hurt and the mood swings. Grown men do cry, feel helpless and despondent and far better to show such feelings, let them wash over you and to seek the comfort, reassurance and support of a loved one.

For our family, James' death signified great love, great loss and great joy. As Julia read to me one morning, again from Julian of Norwich:

> *And although the battle is not won nor the pilgrimage completed, we know that we have sufficient light. This is our source of life. But we cannot escape the suffering and the sorrow: there are dark sides to life. Realism forces us to face the fact. And the same realism enables us to trust the light and life and love in which we are enfolded.*

Losing James changed how I viewed life. So often we take matters for granted and skim over the surface of things – as my brother-in-law said at the funeral, "life is what happens to you when you are making other plans". After the accident, life suddenly became more focused and more intense.

James' gift was to open my eyes and soul to the fullness and richness of life and to allow me to live in the moment; whether listening to magpies warbling in the morning sun, watching the wattle-birds hopping through the camellia bushes outside my study window or seeing morning dew shimmering on a spider's web.

All those years after first reading his poetry at university, I now understood what Blake meant when he wrote in *Auguries of Innocence*: "To see a world in a grain of sand, And a heaven in a wild flower, Hold infinity in the palm of your hand, And eternity in an hour."

In addition to literature, for me, there was also music. I'd always said to James and Amelia that music touches the soul and transports one to a better world. Ever since the accident music has filled the house and it is rare that a day passes in silence.

I'll always remember, as a Year 11 student, being introduced to Bach's Brandenburg Concertos. I had no idea who the composer was, when he had lived or why he was famous – all I knew was that the music moved me profoundly and opened a new world of enjoyment and composure.

One of my favourite poems is Hope's *Vivaldi, Bird and Angel* where the poet describes a bird overhearing Vivaldi's music being played. The bird wonders whether such an ignorant, lowly creature as man can make sounds so pure and sublime:

Why there… and there…
It touched it, it caught it… I could swear
It was indeed our mating song…
Ah, no
It could not be… so clumsy, gross and slow
How could they… yet I wonder… there again!
So different, such strange joy… could things like
men
Know rapture? Sing as birds sometimes sing
For sheer delight?

There is sheer delight in music and compositions like Vaughan William's *The Lark Ascending* and Henryk Gorecki's *Sorrowful Songs* transport one to another place – one that calms the mind and refreshes the spirit. Listening, I realise that I am not alone and that in opening myself to something higher, I share with others the beauty and pain of life.

Listening to requiems, whether John Rutter, Gabriel Fauré or Vivaldi, also became a regular event. The music and singing lifted me into a sublime, lyrical dimension far from the stress and worry of this worldly, day-to-day existence.

There were also songs and singers that James had introduced me to: Sade and Dido, Coldplay and John Mayer, Faithless and Powderfinger. Some nights, after too much to drink, I would crank up the sound, close my eyes and let the sounds and lyrics wash over me – feeling in some way that we were once again together and enjoying the moment.

When flat, I also found release in physical activity. Some months after the hit and run accident, the grief counsellor we met told us that there are times when memories are too painful. Best to work in the garden, wash the windows or paint the fence – anything to get you moving and to shift your mind to something practical and immediate.

It is all right to say to James, not at the moment, leave me alone and return another time.

Talking to the counsellor also gave Julia and me the chance to reveal our feelings openly and without constraint – by sharing the sense of loss and suffering we grew closer and were in a better position to support and help one another.

In the weeks after the accident I avoided the ritual of an early Saturday morning trip to the Victoria Market. In time, I returned and it was amongst the fishmongers, the butchers, the deli shops and veggie stalls that life became more bearable.

I rediscovered enjoyment in cooking – whether kneading and knocking down pizza dough, filleting john dory or making scallop soup, working in the kitchen represents time out.

As previously mentioned, it's not unusual for creative artists, composers, actors and comedians to be depressive and to suffer what Winston Churchill called his black dog. The need to be creative often stems from the need to overcome despondency and for me the outlet is words.

The English poet T. S. Eliot writes in *Four Quartets*:

> *Words strain,*
> *Crack and sometimes break, under the burden,*
> *Under the tension, slip, slide, perish.*
> *Decay with imprecision.*

Writing, whether books, newspaper comment pieces or essays for various publications over the years since James' death, has given me the opportunity to be creative.

Sitting in front of a blank screen, clarifying ideas, marshalling arguments and crafting language is difficult. At the same time it opens a world of ideas, debate and counter argument that is engaging and rewarding. Wrestling with language and ideas allows one to enter a world of activity where deeper worries and concerns fade into the background and no longer dominate one's consciousness.

Part 10

Life Goes On

Eleven years after James' death, I sit in front of a computer typing these words and trying to make sense of what has happened. There is no such thing as closure and once one has experienced such pain, suffering and sadness nothing is ever the same

They say that somebody who loses a limb often feels that it is still there – a phantom that lingers and that will never disappear. Every day I feel James' presence and the need to remain true to his memory.

There are still days when the black dog returns and I feel physically and emotionally drained and life appears senseless and without purpose. Why bother going through the stale and empty routine of filling the space before old age and death?

The anniversary of James' death, his birthday and Christmas are especially painful and nothing will ever change the fact that such occasions bring unwanted memories.

At the same time, life goes on and there are loved ones, family and friends to be with and to share laughter and time together. Nieces and nephews starting their own families and watching Amelia begin her career and establish a relationship prove that the cycle of life continues.

James' schoolmates and childhood friends have also offered comfort and reassurance that not all has been lost.

On seeing them on the morning of James' fatal hit and run accident their grief, confusion and pain were palpable. At his funeral some of his closest friends carried James' coffin and the expressions of their faces are still etched on my mind.

Over the years and months since Bastille Day, 2002 we have kept up contact and many have become dear friends sharing birthdays, engagements, weddings and, more recently, children of their own.

Each year we get together in an unofficial memorial to rekindle the memory of a lost schoolmate and much loved brother and son. Such occasions are bittersweet. To be with them is to be reminded of what we have lost, but at the same time, their laughter, energy and the bond that unites us provides happiness and hope for the future.

If financial hardship puts pressure on a marriage, then there is no doubt that losing a son or daughter represents an almost insurmountable challenge. The intimate, loving bond between a husband and wife expresses itself in having children and there's no doubt that the relationship can be destroyed because of a child's death or similar calamity.

For me, given the type of home I grew up in, losing a son rekindled old fears and uncertainties and made me especially vulnerable, and at times, put pressure on our marriage. Thankfully, Julia provided the patience, understanding and unconditional love that made James' death bearable and gave hope for the future.

While not all would agree with the English playwright John Ford in his description, there is no doubt that a wife can be a saviour:

> *The joys of marriage are the heaven on earth,*
> *Life's paradise, great princess, the soul's quiet,*
> *Sinews of concord, earthly immortality,*

Eternity of pleasures; no restoratives
Like to a constant women.

James' death has changed our marriage and transformed it into something very private and more intimate. As his parents, only we know how intense the suffering and loss is and only we can offer the solace and comfort to each other that makes it bearable.

Amelia also proves to be an endearing and supportive daughter whose love and affection help overcome moments of emptiness and grief.

Amelia is now 29 and like her father and mother has taken up teaching as a career. Watching her overcome and deal with the loss of her brother has been painful, and at times, distressing. Like us, Amelia has felt the intolerable burden of heartbreaking sorrow, and like us, she has sometimes lost her way in a fog of despondency and depression.

Thanks to her courage, determination and inherent goodness she has also been able to remain positive and optimistic. For her, teaching primary age children is to embark on a rewarding career by surrounding herself with the energy and possibilities of new life.

One does not have to be religious or believe in God to appreciate that there is evil in the world and that darkness can easily descend on any of us and that the black dog can come barking at our door.

At the same time, for me, the journey since that fateful night has taught me that along side sadness and loss can exist hope, light and optimism.

As noted by Austin Cooper in *Julian of Norwich: Reflection on Selected Texts*, the belief that there is darkness in the world should never overwhelm the reality that there is also light. A light signifying love and acceptance that overcomes adversity and pain:

> *There is an interplay of light and darkness in*
> *ourselves and in our world. We are faced with*
> *conflict and division within, and the conflict*
> *between good and evil in the cosmos. There is need*
> *for mercy and healing.*

The experience has also taught me that men, especially, need to express their sorrow and loss openly and without the fear of being thought weak or unmanly. Sharing emotions, thoughts and feelings with others, especially loved ones, is crucial if one is to escape the slough of despondency.

I also realised my past experiences when growing up as a child in Broadmeadows, no matter how painful or distressing, have helped me deal with James' loss. Out of pain and hardship an inner strength and resilience can be born.

As to what the future brings, given what happened on Bastille Day, 2002, who knows what is yet to come or what fate has in mind. For the three of us to have come so far, though, suggests that there is cause for optimism. While a person cannot control his or her destiny, we all have the ability to be resilient, and with the love, sympathy and support of others, to deal with anxiety and loss.

The lines from Shakespeare's *King Lear*: "Men must endure their going hence, even as their coming hither. Ripeness is all" comes to mind.

On a lighter note, every now and then, and for no apparent reason, I remember the song from the final scene of Monty Python's 'Life of Brian': *Always look on the bright side of life.*

Part 11

A Layman's Guide to Dealing with Depression

[T]hose suffering from cancer are often fortunate enough to be granted remission, but ever present is the fear that death can still come knocking.

Depression is similar, some days are positive and time passes quickly while on other days despair and gloom return and all seems lost and life appears without meaning.

For me, as with Julia and Amelia, James always will be close and the memory of his death is seared into our consciousness and will never be erased. As previously mentioned, there is no such thing as closure.

The challenge for me, and for others who have experienced suffering and loss, is to tame Churchill's black dog and to gain some semblance of normalcy, to keep on an even keel and to recommit to a life worth living.

While not an expert on dealing with depression, based on my experience and the experience of those I love most, it is possible to make some suggestions:

1. For men, in particular, it is vital to express and to share with others the pain and suffering caused by the death of a loved one or the impact of other life changing events. Bottling up your thoughts and emotions on the pretext that you must be stoic

and in control only leads to greater suffering.

2. Seek the help of professionals and don't be afraid to admit the seriousness of how debilitating depression can be. Psychologists and grief counsellors, in addition to giving practical advice, also know the various stages of pain, anxiety and loss and can provide vital advice and a much needed clinical perspective.

3. Realise that there are different stages of depression and loss – shock, anger, denial, anguish, weariness, resignation and acceptance – and understand that while time does not heal completely, its passing can provide a better and more balanced perspective.

4. Understand that depression can distort and colour how you view life and relate to others. Anxiety and suffering can make you irritable and short tempered and turn you against the ones who love you most and who are in the best position to help.

5. Make time to be physical, to be active and to give yourself a break from the daily routine – especially, when the black dog draws close. As research has proven, physical exercise releases endorphins that have a positive impact.

6. Beware of seeking to escape in negative and destructive behaviour – as anyone who has got drunk or taken drugs knows, the problem is still there the day after, and if anything, has only been made worse.

7. Understand that there are larger forces at work – fate, destiny, God – and that it is often easier to give yourself up to something higher than to struggle and fight against what might be inevitable.

8. While the expression 'life wasn't meant to be easy' is glib, it expresses an essential truth. Accept the fact, while we all prefer happiness, that to be human is to be vulnerable to pain and suffering.

9. Understand that it is a test of character to deal with and overcome depression and to tame the black dog. We all have free will and the power to choose.

10. Realise that depression can be channelled into something positive – some of the most creative artists, composers, actors, thinkers, and successful public figures and politicians have suffered depression.

11. Seek solace and help in whatever reveals the wonder, beauty and mystery of life and that affirms something beneficial and positive. Whether art, music, literature, nature or the love and friendship of others.